THE UNFORGETABLE SISTER..

ANUSHKA CHAKRABORTY

Copyright © Anushka Chakraborty
All Rights Reserved.

ISBN 979-888591018-7

This book has been published with all efforts taken to make the material error-free after the consent of the author. However, the author and the publisher do not assume and hereby disclaim any liability to any party for any loss, damage, or disruption caused by errors or omissions, whether such errors or omissions result from negligence, accident, or any other cause.

While every effort has been made to avoid any mistake or omission, this publication is being sold on the condition and understanding that neither the author nor the publishers or printers would be liable in any manner to any person by reason of any mistake or omission in this publication or for any action taken or omitted to be taken or advice rendered or accepted on the basis of this work. For any defect in printing or binding the publishers will be liable only to replace the defective copy by another copy of this work then available.

For there is no friend like a sisterIn calm or stormy weather; To cheer one on the tedious way, To fetch one if one goes astray,To lift one if one totters down, To strengthen whilst one stands. So this story dedicates my elder sister who's going to get married soon and I am going to miss her a lot. No matter how many years passed or how much responsibility each assumed, they still managed to bicker like bitchy teenagers on a regular basis. In some way, though, each found it comforting; it reminded them how close they really were: Acquaintances were always on their best behavior, but sisters loved each other enough to say anything. This quote by Lauren Weisberger really makes me emotional..

Contents

FOREWORD

She's someone you can confide in about family matters. She already understands and knows the pain.She'll be there no matter what—even if the two of you were just in a fight yesterday.She knows all of the songs you secretly like but don't tell anyone about, so it's completely acceptable to turn it up and belt it out in the car with her.She'll push you out of your comfort zone, and even though you'll kick and scream the entire time, you are secretly grateful for it and she is a sister. This book is regarding a sissy bond only..

PREFACE

She'll tell you not to buy another tank top, because she knows you already have 12 in the closet. And no, it doesn't matter how cute you think this particular tank top is. You can always count on her to try and talk you out of a bad idea even though you've never listened in the past.She can say just one word to make you laugh uncontrollably, and it's the Wait-Stop-I-Can't-Breathe-And-My-Abs-Are-On-Fire kind of laugh and this sister bonding story must be liked and loved by you all..

Acknowledgements

I would like to express my parents who inspired me to write at such a young on this cute sissy bond that is regarding marriage of a sister and her parting from the younger one..You are the one person I have always been able to count on and I love you more with each year that passes, my first and dearest friend. Sister, no matter how old we get, being with you is like being a little girl again. The best gift Mom and Dad ever gave me was you. She's not just my best friend; she's my sister.They are relationships in which love and rivalry – as well as envy and empathy – coexist, if not always easily. Sisters know each other inside out. They know better than anyone else each other's hopes and dreams – and, as Amy proves, they also know precisely what to do and what to say in order to wound one another.Thank you, forever and ever, for a feeling of belonging and unity I could never get anywhere else. I love you so deeply, and so fully, from the bottom of my heart. To my sister, thank you for being there whenever I needed a helping hand. Thank you for always being honest.

Prologue

Her prominence is more subtle.

Sure, she's your sister, and could even be one of your best friends, but she's so much more than that.

If you have a close relationship with your sister, you should feel so fortunate, because you really hit the jackpot in the sibling department.

I

INTRODUCTION TO THE SISSY BOND

Do you know why sisters are the best ?

THIS IS MY SISTER SONALI..

Here are fifty - two reasons for the same..
1. You always have good jokes
2. Your always make sure my water bottle is full before you go to bed
3. We watch the same TV shows
4. You like the breakfast I cook, even when you have to eat alone
5. You always do cool things to my hair, even though it's very short
6. You are a best friend that I was born with
7. You're always good for a laugh
8. You always let me shower first so my shower can be warm
9. I can always rely on you
10. You like to play with fun toys
11. You're still truly a kid at heart, even though you are 23. Yes, 23.
12. You took care of me when I cried in the middle of the night
13. You taught me to read, just not to pronounce the words I read
14. You taught me to be responsible
15. You always let me borrow your clothes, even when you don't know I have them
16. You're always on my side
17. You always do funny things, like making reusable paper towels
18. I love your face when you fart in my room and then walk away
19. Your burps make the dinner table a unique place
20. You love my brownies, even when I cook them a normal

person amount

21. You always share a pot of mac and cheese with me

22. You let me drive on Sunday mornings even though it makes you carsick

23. You always tell me when I'm wrong

24. I love the amount you've taught me about myself and always believing in myself

25. I love how honest you always are and how you always tell me how it is and how I'm acting

26. You went through everything first so I wouldn't have to

27. You always traded carrots and green beans with me when we thought mom and dad weren't looking

28. In 5 years, I want to be just like you. But not look like you. That would be creepy

29. You've always been a role model. I look up to you

30. You always know how to have fun

31. You're always so creative

32. You tell me how it is, you don't sugar coat things for me

33. You used to let me do your homework so I wouldn't be bored.

34. I can always depend on you, no matter what

35. You like to try new things every day

36. You let me borrow your shoes, even when you were gonna wear them already

37. You don't tickle me

38. You're always concerned about my well being

39. You always know what to say to people to make them like you

40. You paint my toenails

41. You always stood up for me

42. You don't get upset that people think I'm the older one

43. You inspired me to swim my hardest and to reach for my goals until I reached them

44. You're always there to lend me a hand, especially when I need it the most
45. You've accepted my friends as your friends, and treat them like your own sisters
46. I love that you're a true friend, and that you're with me till the end
47. You're so pretty, even when you just wake up
48. You always say what's on your mind, even when it doesn't really make sense
49. You got all the hair. I don't have to deal with having too much now
50. You weren't allowed to name me Tina.
51. You accept me for who I am, even when I'm irrational and crazy
52. You'll always love me, whether or not we live in a duplex

If you were asked to name the most important person in your life, you may say your mom, your dad, or even your best friend. But don't ever underestimate the bond of a great sisterhood.

Your sister may not be the first one to come to mind because the reasons she's important aren't so obvious.

Her prominence is more subtle.

Sure, she's your sister, and could even be one of your best friends, but she's so much more than that.

If you have a close relationship with your sister, you should feel so fortunate, because you really hit the jackpot in the sibling department.

She is my sister who is going to leave me soon for her marriage..

She used to teach me every subject so beautifully that I didn't need any other outsider for teaching me.

She is the best sister ever. She is going to get married and I'll be missing her a lot..

II

SISSY INFORMATIONS

For there is no friend like a sisterIn calm or stormy weather; To cheer one on the tedious way, To fetch one if one goes astray,To lift one if one totters down, To strengthen whilst one stands. So this story dedicates my elder sister who's going to get married soon and I am going to miss her a lot. No matter how many years passed or how much responsibility each assumed, they still managed to bicker like bitchy teenagers on a regular basis. This is in case of my sissy. If she gets married I'll be alone. Yet there is nothing to do. Every one has to get married at a age and leave for a new home.Sisterhood is a bond forged of paper, stone, steel, blood and Kryptonite. And nothing could be more precious.Sisters can be maddening. They take you for granted and make unfair demands and push your buttons like nobody else. They say things to you that in a million years they wouldn't dream of saying to their friends, in-laws or colleagues. And when they're not happy or feeling insecure, you as perhaps their closest-looking and -living relative can be the recipient of their unintentional projections.Depending on your closeness — and how much therapy you've both had — you might be able to discuss this in an objective, loving, helpful way. Or it could stew for days, weeks, months or, tragically, it could be the undoing of your entire relationship.

Do you know how are sisters beneficial?

1. They do wonders for your mental health.

All those years of squabbling have finally paid off. One report that followed 571 families found that having a sister means you will generally score higher on the standard range of tests for good mental health.
The psychologists discovered people who grew up with at least one sister were less anxious and less likely to have depression. It seems this is all a consequence of the fact sisters help foster communication and generally make their siblings more comfortable with their emotions.

2. They make you happy.

A study from Brigham Young University shows that positive sibling relationships — particularly sisters — have lasting positive effects on your happiness levels. The close bonds encourage traits like kindness and generosity, which continue into adult life.
3. They make you smart.

Yep, sisters make you more intelligent, according to research from Concordia University. They found that sisters teach us in a similar way that teachers do, and we learn more growing up through the initiation of the activities that they involve us in.
4. They make you strong.

2009 research carried out by the Psychologists at the University of Ulster and De Monfort University found that having a sister means you're less susceptible to suffering from stressful situations later in your life.

Co-author of the study, University of Ulster researcher Tony Cassidy, said sisters promote "emotional expression":

"Our explanation for it is that the presence of girls opens up channels of communication and it becomes a much more expressive situation that's positive."

5. She makes you a better listener.

Apparently men who grow up with sisters are much better listeners and are also better at talking to women. In his research about sibling relationships, The Sibling Effect, Jeffrey Kluger discovered that when you pair people up in five to 15 minute conversations, males who grew up with sisters tended to do better than men who grew up with brothers, or as only children.

Thank you Mamamia for giving me all these information so that I can feel that I am blessed to have a sister..

III

THE SISSY FEELINGS

Siblings are important for many reasons. First, given their closeness in age, kids may be more likely to tell their siblings things that they might not tell their parents. Second, given that children and teenagers are more likely to confide in their siblings, they may also turn more readily to their siblings as a source of support. This piece is critical, because we know that one of the biggest risk factors for developing youth is suffering in isolation. The ability for young people to express their feelings to anyone - sibling, parent, or friend - can be highly therapeutic and can prevent a worsening of depressed mood or anxiety. Finally, siblings can serve as a sounding board for one another before trying things out in social settings. There is evidence to suggest that healthy sibling relationships promote empathy, prosocial behavior and academic achievement.Another source of stress can be when adults compare one sibling to another. This has the dual effect of shattering the self-esteem of the sibling who feels judged, while driving a wedge between the siblings and pushing them further apart. Also, when one sibling is suffering medically or emotionally, it can be a considerable stressor for the entire household including other siblings.

Brothers and sisters are each other's superheroes with super-healing powers; consider yourself lucky to have them.

Like sugar and spice, siblings make things extra nice.

Friends come and go, but brothers (sisters) are forever.

It's OK to lean on your siblings in times of need, they have both the strongest and the softest shoulders to cry on.

Siblings know how to push each other's buttons, but they also know how to mend things faster than anyone.

Your sister (brother) is your real life guardian angel, you just can't see their wings.

And all these qualities are posessed in my sister..

Siblings are put on this Earth to love, to entertain, and to annoy each other. It's part of their job requirements.

If it wasn't for you, I wouldn't have anyone to blame my mistakes on.

Sometimes sweet, sometimes sour, you can always count on your brothers and sisters to give you variety.

Only you know and keep all of my secrets, because if you don't, I will tell yours.

Sharing, I mean stealing, each other's things is the best part about having a brother (sister).

Only siblings know the fear of calling "shotgun" last, to see who gets the front car seat first.

My brother is the only one who will tell me when an outfit makes me look fat. Even when it doesn't!

Even these funny phrases describe her..

Also,Having grown up in a family with a sister on your side is the living proof of a constant support. Although chemistries do change according to the relationship (a sister-to-sister background is often different to a brother-to-sister photo album), one thing is more than certain: your sister has always been there for you, either as the mirror of your virtues and your inconsistencies (we have to admit we all have some) or as a symbol of affection and unconditional love

Also sisters are very cool. We can share all our feelings with them without any hesitance that we hesitate to tell our parents. Even sisters do not tell the facts we tell them to our parents otherwise may be today we've been beaten by our parents. So, it's really necessary to have sister and if you don't have adopt one and try to strengthen your bond with her.

IV
SISTER BONDINGS

Sisters are best friends, they are advisors, they are teachers, and best of all they are people with whom you can talk with about anything - someone you have a special bond with! This famous quote by Catherine Pulsifer really tends to make sister bond even stronger.

I have got information about a reasons why big sisters are thr amazing. Wanna know it?

She took all the flak from your parents so you didn't have to.

While being the eldest child does have its high points, as your big sister will be the first to remind you, it has a lot of low points too.

Your older sister was there first (duh), so she was the one that your parents focused all of their worry and paranoia on. She was the one who got in a ton of trouble for a "C" on her report card, whereas you got a pat on the back and, "Do better next semester."

She was the one who got yelled at for staying out late,

whereas you just slipped in the back door without the slightest reprimand.

She was the one who was pressured to major in a "practical" field in college when she didn't want to. You got away with majoring in basket weaving.Parents tend to "mellow out" a bit with their younger children. Why? Your older sister proved that you could get a low grade, stay out late, and major in what you want to without your life falling to pieces. She did all the hard work of getting things into perspective for your parents so you didn't have to. You owe her a big thank-you for that!

My sister is really kind and honest beacause my sister and I are bonded for life. I have to be honest with her when she asks for advice, although it may mean giving her some tough love. Tough love and trust is what helps the relationship to grow stronger everyday.

Do you know some reasons why I love my sister?

Couldn't get through Latin 1? If your sister took it the year before, she was the one helping you learn the difference between a declension and a conjugation. Struggled through Algebra 2? Your sister was probably the one who sat down with you a helped you figure out the functions on your graphing calculator.

She warned you what types of questions were going to be on the SAT or ACT, and she told you what the transition into college would be like. Getting through school is a heck of a lot less scary if you have someone around who has already passed all your classes!

For example, maybe you got some of her old teachers—hopefully teachers who liked her! They saw your last name and immediately warmed to you, especially when they found out who your older sister was. A little bit of favoritism on your side never goes amiss.

Chances are your sister also warned you about which teachers were going to give you grief, and maybe gave you some advice for not ticking them off. That indispensable advice could make all the difference in the world.

When you first started in secondary school, maybe she was the one who also told you which foods were utterly inedible in the cafeteria, and which part of the hallway to avoid if you didn't want to get shoved in your own locker.

If your sister went to college ahead of you, she could give you some great advice on your college applications, and maybe more importantly, your search for the perfect school. She was able to provide perspective not just on academics, but also on student life. She could tell you all about sports, clubs, sororities, and other aspects of campus life which may or may not have been in your college brochures.

If you followed in your sister's footsteps in the professional world and not just in your education, she might have been one of your earliest job references. A reference from an older sister is a great way to get your foot in the door at your first internship or first job.

Employers felt like they already had a pretty good grasp of what working with you might be like. And if you ended up in the same office, it was your older sister who showed you the ropes and mentored you in your new job role!

Maybe you took after your parents when it came to fashion, but maybe not. If your older sister didn't, she showed you a whole new way to dress. And unlike your parents, she was with it when it came to the times!

She was the one who saved you from going out in that awful sweater your mother tried to make you wear, and let you borrow that cute top. She let you sneak off to that party in her favorite stiletto heels, did your makeup for you, and transformed you into the coolest kid on the block.kpopociousss

If you had too much to drink at that party, your parents never found out, thanks to your older sister who drove you home and made an excuse for you at the door so you could head off to sleep before they picked up on your inebriated state.

When you got in trouble at school, but it didn't warrant a call to your parents, it was your sister who chose to keep her mouth shut at home. Think how much harder it would have been to get through those situations if you'd been on your own!

Since your sister had more experience with Mom and Dad than you, she was able to teach you exactly what you needed to do in order to get away with doing what you wanted.

She was the one who told you whether it was best to take a stand or lie low, or if there was a certain way you could phrase a request so that you'd get a pass.

She let you know exactly where the line was and when you would be crossing it. She learned all of this stuff the hard way so you didn't have to.

THIS IS US..

When your parents went out and left you home with your older sister, she was your babysitter. Maybe she didn't like it all of the time, but it was the perfect time to introduce you to her favorite movies or music or do your makeup. And she cooked for you!

Her food probably wasn't gourmet, but sometimes you don't want gourmet. Sometimes you want macaroni and cheese and cookies and milk. And she didn't try to take the cookies away from you before you'd had your fill. And only you could appreciate each others' bizarre culinary experiments.

If your parents came down on you for something unfair, your older sister may have stuck up for you now and again, especially if it was something she herself got away with.

Whether she presented a strong case on your side or acted as an arbiter, she stepped in on your behalf. She may not always have done a great job of it, but it was the thought that counted, and just think where you'd have been without her.

Okay, well, this depends totally on how popular she was. But if your older sister was considered a pretty exciting person at school, odds were that a little bit of that automatically rubbed off on you. Hopefully it was enough to get you into the right social circles without overshadowing you completely.

Maybe some of her friends also became your friends. And if a bunch of juniors or seniors thought you were "all right" as a freshman, well, that was definitely something. Any freshman with friends in older classes is just going to be respected by default.

Your older sister is someone who can look back with you and reminisce on the past. She shares a lot of your best memories of childhood and a lot of your worst ones too. If you are trying to cope with something painful from your past, she is there to give you some perspective.

She can understand all of the little neuroses you carry with you because of your upbringing better than most. But she also remembers the good stuff, and can still laugh at the private joke you shared when you were still in elementary school together.

Your big sister is someone who will be connected to you for the rest of your life, both by blood and by all the memories that you share. No matter where life takes you, you'll always have someone you can call to talk to about the past or about the present.

Hopefully you'll be able to get together a few times a year, or if you live close, maybe you'll get to hang out every week! Either way, your big sister will always be there for you, a friend and role model forever